WINTER INLET

WINTER INLET

Hastings Hensel

Winner of the Unicorn Press First Book Award

UNICORN PRESS

GREENSBORO 2015

First printing

ISBN 978-0-87775-937-9 (paperback)
ISBN 978-0-87775-938-6 (cloth)

EPIGRAPHS: The excerpt from Seamus Heaney's essay "Mossbawn" first appeared in *Finders Keepers: Selected Prose 1971-2001* (Faber & Faber, 2003). The excerpt from Philip Larkin's "Aubade" first appeared in *Collected Poems* (Farrar, Straus, Giroux; 2004). The excerpt from Rafil Kroll-Zaidi first appeared in his "Findings" column in the May 2012 issue of *Harper's Magazine*.

COVER IMAGE: "Fishing with a Remora as Described by Columbus" first appeared in Conrad Gesner's *Historiæ Animalium* and is reproduced here from the *Annual Report of the Board of Regents of the Smithsonian Institution*, 1848.

∞

This book is printed on Mohawk Via, which is acid-free and meets ANSI standards for archival permanence.

Unicorn Press
1212 Grove Street
Greensboro, NC 27403

www.unicorn-press.org

Grateful acknowledgement is made to the editors of the journals
in which some of these poems, occasionally in different versions,
first appeared: *Connotation Press: An Online Artifact*, *32 Poems*,
Cave Wall, *Sheepshead Review*, *storySouth*, *Fall Lines: Poetry
of the Rough South*, *The Greensboro Review*, *Steel Toe Review*,
Birmingham Poetry Review, and in a limited-edition chapbook,
Control Burn, published by *Iron Horse Literary Review*.

I would also like to thank the following people, many of whom
offered wisdom and insight while I wrote these poems, and
without whom there would be no poetry at all: my family, for
their stories; my teachers Dave Smith, Mary Jo Salter, Andrew
Hudgins, and John Irwin; the entire Sewanee Writers' Conference
staff and all my friends from Johns Hopkins University; everyone
in the English departments at The University of the South
and Coastal Carolina University; the good people at the South
Carolina Arts Commission, for a fellowship; William Logan and
Maurice Manning, for close reads; my friends Will Griffin, Jolly
Roger, Shane Gage, Jonathan Heinen, James Thomas Miller, and
Adam Vines, for continued inspiration and good times.

But especially: Wyatt Prunty and Paul Ragan.

for Lee

We passed the ice of pain,
And came to a dark ravine,
And there we sang with the sea:
The wide, the bleak abyss
Shifted with our slow kiss.

ROETHKE

WINTER INLET

WINTER INLET

ON THE FAR SHORE

Across the oxbow
I saw what I thought
    was fallen cypress,
though rowing closer

    I discovered
hunkered gators
    who turned again
into old canoes,

ivy-covered, disused.
    On the far shore
I flipped one over,
    and what I thought

I should have seen—
    a moccasin, cocked
back to strike—
    I didn't see, but saw

instead a black line
    that coiled and climbed
over the gunwales
    and turned into vine.

ONE

WINTER INLET ARRANGEMENT

Is everything pain? Scar lines and scrapes
of gray cloud, gull scream, crushed shells
slicing the tin sheen of the pluff mudbank.
Pained: a bloated rib cage of marsh grass
floating by on the wind-stitched surface,
rock jetties accepting their punishment,
assaulted by salt spray, without objection,
bullish oystermen kneeling in the low tide.

False spring heals nothing. All remains in pain:
clear water, starved, and in it the stone crab
waving its heavy claw for help. Even the tide
in pain: roaring in, screaming out. A cold rain
falls on the empty traps. No flounder lie flat
in the honey holes. Cannonball jellyfish explode.

SPIGOT

"There the pump stands...marking the centre of
another world." SEAMUS HEANEY

Ordered toward that quiet space
of snakes where the yard hose
snakes past the mole that lies
thrillingly dead in the ant bed,
and a puzzle of ivy shadows
riddles the cracked cinder block
walls of the house, I followed—
without question—the question-
marked hose, past each prickly
holly bush and a manic rush
of insects, to this other world
where a spigot handle bloomed
out of the pipe in the ground.
My uncle swung the nozzle,
pistol-whipping air, hollered,
Let there be water! and so there
I let water be: three twanged
clockwise cranks of the handle,
and water flowed like language
from my world to that other,
to where he stood by the boat,
washing the new world's words:
bow, rudder, batten, transom, stern.

GOUGING FOR GLASS

With my iron rod
I bend down low
and prod the mud
at dead low tide,

below the salt wind
and the marsh grass
the salt wind strums,
gouging for glass.

I think it must clink
like a typewriter key
after a long pause
in which no thought

worth its salt comes.
I have marked the rod
with lines, the times.
Oh, everywhere I go

I puncture the earth
like the egret does:
footprint, rod hole,
period and comma.

Once I hit a dead fish.
Heron bone, an anchor.
But never anything
I keep gouging after:

shards of amber, jade,
frosted Kelly greens.
A jar, cornflower blue,
inches, decades, down.

HUMAN IMPRINT

The baby vulture, captured,
imagined me as I was:
mother, lover, rival.

Call it an existential crisis.
The nest I'd found
out prowling the woods

should never have fallen,
but it nearly
fell into my arms.

A real mother hovered
upwards, rocked
on the thin air above the river.

Call it a moral quandary
if you must, but just
think about it first:

the very first thing effective
at love she saw,
yes, was me.

Think positive psychology.
All this vulture
could learn about nurture,

I taught her: how to laugh
like a drunk in the afternoons,
how to touch

softly the back of a neck.
And nature:
that jealousy is rage,

but rage, like passion, dies down.
Once, set free,
she rebuffed the hospitable air.

Call her scatterbrained,
purblind.
I named her Angeline,

and Angeline limped back
to my doorstep and pecked
at my back door glass.

When I shot her, her neck
writhed like a rattlesnake
alive in the grass.

GO-DEVIL

a 9-pound firewood-splitting maul; for P.R.

Blunt-headed and stubborn
      as a non believer,
wedged into oak beside
      the snow-capped
trash pile on a cold day
      with a sky brushed
back by clouds, the sun
      splintering the jagged
crack of the horizon.
      Plain dumb, that's one
way the devil plays you,
      and here he comes,
your old man ambling
      from cabin to shed,
then into the woods
      thick with hemlock
branches he'll split
      with it, then nothing
but old hands that drag
      the tracks deeply back
to where he pulls the tool
      out of the stump
and pumps his old
      arms up and down,
smiting oak like a sin
      he's long forgotten.

A SCHOOL OF MULLET

Netless I strolled the bank
    to scrutinize how
        ray-finned
they coursed the current
    so disciplined in the functional thrill

of jumping
    of puncturing surface that when

they approached the creek's bend
    in context
I could feel each body
        uncritical and silvery
    a flash
        break apart
    as my shadow broke them
        the one school
        how it split
as the creek at the sandbar splits

    and comes back together

like a lesson to take from it all
    though I didn't take it

        but instead I raised my head to see

a wavering *V* of geese
        rupture a cloud
    and that was like a mouth
opening and closing

        a mouth
that makes the sound
        of water gurgling where

    the school of mullet and all its knowledge
        pass

MEN-OF-WAR

Such viscous discs
    washed up on the beach,

prodded by a dune reed,
    notched by gull beaks,

glinting in the brown sand
    like wet coins for some bullet-

nicked insurgent's son
    to come pickpocketing the dead

before he swaggers forth
    from the ecstasy of wreckage.

A man too long at war might
    see something vibrantly sexual—

the thin pink edge, blue tentacles
    from which black flies spin off,

white breaker foam nudging
    like a tongue. Or just disgust:

a brainy nonbrain remaining like
    an eye degenerated—blind but open.

MAN WHO TALKS TO PELICANS

Our little fishing village Doolittle
struts the docks with his bucket
of fish guts he chucks in the creek,
as all the seagulls seem to scream
with joy and all the mullet nearly
roll over the surface with laughter.
We swear the sawgrass draws back
like a curtain for when they come:
the abstract, observant pelicans.

What doesn't he say to this one
pouching a fileted winter trout?
This one, he swears, by the look
in her eyes, is definitely a lady.
Of blazons he could talk all day.
Her hair? Slicked back and coiffed
just like his first crush, Doris Day.
Her eyes? Bejeweled obsidian.
Her neck? Sexier than Cleopatra's.

Gently he pets their wet heads
and then says, *Be kind to our kind*,
repeating such easy moral pleas
that none of us dare walk away.
They too stay, circling the surface,
unsated and sad as our wild side-
showman of the marsh docks stops,
accepts their shy goodbyes, and
turns back towards the cruel land.

HAVING REMEMBERED AN ICE STORM

Stir-crazy, staring out like cats at
that view to die for, which, encased,
    seemed to have died—

the oak trees, frozen, never stirring
when the wind came, nor any music
    from the chimes.

Everywhere the smell of fresh pines
where their limbs had splintered,
    and jays zipped by.

And before the thaw, what we thought
was snow, though it was only whitecaps
    that lifted into gulls

pulled into a sky full of cumuli
that, you said, looked like old
    tortoises…slow

and purposeful in their changes.
What else but memory rearranges
    a year, a day

on the near shore where a kite
plummets to become sail, then
    a heron, breezeblown

on the back lawn, then
a moth I find rummaging among
    your summer things?

NIGHT JETTY

Still when we sleep the sleek
spindrift-pitched
rock jetty lifts the salt spray,

prints white the black night
a madness—this
that, nonetheless without us,

persists. But it's not exactly
the dreaminess
the fish possess, finning past

what seem like giant's teeth,
high tide-sheathed,
some Jurassic spine reclined,

deepening the dark channel
where they swim,
closer, but as quiet as the stars.

FILET

The thin blade bends
   in fish skin,
saws along the shoulder,
    fins, extends
through belly and breast,
    comes clean out
the other side, sweeps
    in air where
the eye has hardened
    to a marble,
and the entrails then
    spill, the guts
erupt, and gray lungs
    plunge out
until the slippery rip
    riding of spine—
each blade stroke flat
    in one direction
over the smaller bones
    like fretwork—
pulling skin, pushing
    the knife ahead
to hold, then, the limp
    flimsy filet
free, but dully limpid
    like memory,
or ice. Then the stray
    shards of bone
discarded, the blood
    flecks washed
away from the smooth
    grooves of vein.

CLEANING CRAB IN THE ERA OF BIG DATA

I crack back the carapace,
pry it open with thumbnail,

knife blade, rummage through
gut mustard and trashed lungs

in a hunt for clean meat among
such simple things: a back porch

in spring, cold beer and butter
on a wicker table covered over

with summer's breaking news.
Spies, they gather in the shells,

the dark eyes, in little antennae.
They watch us, even in our joy.

LATE SPRING INLET ARRANGEMENT

Still all is tidal: an influx of cash,
new fish, how the winter grass

dies and sandflies arise out of
the brown-green marsh. Gulls,

like tourists, wade dully along
a buffet of shoreline. Still tidal:

the wide white wakes of boats
beneath golden cumuli drifting

in an unthreatening sky where
black specks, tern flocks, bank

then wheel as if on an invisible
half-pipe. Coming in, going out:

the parasails filling like poppies,
the fiddlers and their curtain calls.

BY-CATCH

Not the almighty succulent shrimp
hand-picked like jewels from the pile
hauled in and dumped by the trawl,

nor even the clichéd rubber boot,
nor the terrified and pathetic dolphin.
Not Ophelia in her muddy dress,

her mouth forever opened in song,
yet still it meant money: square grouper,
the deck crew coined their by-catch

when they withdrew from the ocean
two fifty-five-gallon drums of cocaine.
But even then no long moral debate,

nor any predicament about what to do.
This was it: an exit from the stench-work
of fish guts and salt-covered waders,

seagulls forever screaming behind them
like a requiem for lives of prosperity.
So the crew sold it all summer and waded

in the money. We know what we are, but
know not what we may be, Ophelia mumbled
before her leap into the river, and who

among them thought they'd be caught
like shrimp or dolphin or rubber boots
in the profiteering nets of the law?

GEORGETOWN COUNTY PLANTATION BOAT TOUR

I throttled forth
from the public landing,
alone in my johnboat,

steering to where
the property names
hung resplendent

in the muggy air—
Guendalos, Chicora Wood,
Prospect Hill,

where the caretakers,
winding and rewinding
their lawn mowers

over the checkered
grass, declined
to wave back,

as though I looked
like the kind of man
willing to trespass—

to anchor up
and belly down on
the youngest daughter

in a sweet tea light
unwinding under
the azalea bushes

or, sinking myself
in a hammock
as banked clouds

reclined, reread
(out loud)
all of Faulkner,

or waltz the widow's
walk beneath
the rice-white moon,

or talk for hours
of my wasted life,
reciting my poems.

Privilege enough,
it's true, to know
the sunlit river,

and I motored past
as though I could
let daydreams

flash, then flinch,
be gone forever
like goldfinches

fluttering their wings
beside the wide,
bright windows

of those sunrooms
where our lives would differ,
be better, even the weather,

shadows on the lawn,
dusk, then dawn,
the yawning afternoons

I'd walk among
those oak trees
with their own histories.

WIDOWMAKER

Stump the high tide hides,
driftwood the floods bring—

the river fisherman's kenning
for when he comes screaming

down the one river he's known
longer than his own signature.

Dark, unseen. Like a thought
I should have further explained.

Let me explain: I am exhausted
always weaving between meanings,

trying to gauge timing and depth.
When I look closer, there's a man

whose arms surface and reach out
of the blue to you, after my death.

SNAG ARRANGEMENT

Everything ornamental and forlorn:
plugs hung up in the limb clutch,
plastic worms wrapped around
and squirming from the power lines,
spinner baits stuck in the stumps.
Everything snatched up: foul hooks
by snot-grass clumps and mud-sunk
brush piles, jigs in the oyster beds.

Everything fragmented, faithless:
never the fish one wished for more
than God. Everything suspended
in the upside down—miscast as if
one mistook a clear sky for water
and went out fishing for the birds.

THE OYSTER CLEANING CAGE

Shell-chomp and burp of salt stench.
To feed ourselves, first we'd feed it:
the hand-cranked, rusted-iron barrel

beneath the mildewed green roof
of the boat wash where we'd cruise to
after puttering in the falling tide,

hammering fresh clusters of oysters
illegally from the marsh. The old salts
taught me how to aim the spray gun,

while one of them spun the bucket load,
and we'd watch pluff mud rain down,
uncloaking the barnacle-gray blades.

This cage, it makes individuals of us all,
Big Toady joked—because of the way
it busted up clusters into single selects

that he would shuck open at the heel,
top with Bacos, pre-packaged Hollandaise,
call *Oyster Jolly Rogerfeller*. All winter

that Falstaffian fishing captain starved
for work but ate for free what he caught
in the creek. Another, Shotgun Shane,

bitched at the rich for marking up
shrimp and grits, green tomatoes, ribs.
The joke now: you bought Twinkies

to feed the kids. *Were't not for laughing,*
the prince said of Falstaff, *I should pity him.*
But who could mention pity back then?

The money, like fish, we knew would come
back in the spring. Fresh scars would arc
like hooks, then thin white. Old Dooley,

with his turtle limp, and his food stamps,
would go and buy a dozen lobster tails
and a box of Saltines. We'd eat like kings.

CONVERSION NARRATIVE IN A WALK-IN FREEZER

I staggered, bourbon-haggard, inside,
hoping to sober up as the door swung

shut. Outside, the other men gathered
around their laughter as if it were fire.

Frigid crypt of field-dressed, headless,
gutted bucks with back straps stripped,

each hooked and strung up like Christ,
haunches hanging over nauseous me.

I slid down, shivered, spun and woke
suspended by my belt on a meat hook,

at a height where each white underbelly
I now saw as a field stiffened with snow,

and, below, each antler a leaf-stripped
winter tree, a river-worn eye of stone.

There I came to, knew, bare-bone chill,
as outside, with laughter, men burned.

OLD MEN PARKED AT THE LANDING

Alone in the dark of my condo,
I look down to where their taillights
smolder in the creeping dawn.

I too could gaze out at that view,
one says, to die for—our inlet shore—
but watch them as they idle there,

nearly motionless, shadowy as fish.
My old man was one of them once,
slumped in his clunky black Ford.

Out looking for jobs, finding none,
he'd park and work the crossword,
then, when done, come home at five.

Some day I'll go down there to think
of him—and those years as water,
and not as dirt packed hard with lies.

A CASE AGAIN FOR SOLIPSISM

In the winter inlet my clam rake scrapes
the shell bank's mud, and each littleneck

is a baby's fists clunking inside my bucket.
All day I'm under no sun, turning ground,

no one around except the plovers blown
away by the cold wind, the laughing gull

who stands like a man beside the water—
a man who isn't remembering his mother.

Mostly it's just the broken husks of crabs,
the waves chomping at the bit—nothing

to forget come spring, when rare clusters
of starfish wash up again like old dreams.

NEXT SUMMER INLET ARRANGEMENT

Umbrellas will open up to their fullest selves,
and there will never have been a day so hot,
when porpoises will leap higher than clouds
that are just about to burst with happiness.

Everyone will be dying to get out there
where the breaker foam nudges our ankles
like the cutest puppy. And if you're not happy,
then jump off the highest cliff you can find,

and take your poetry. Oh we'll be happy
to show you the way, beer in hand, but why
miss that day—the best it'll have ever been?

THEORY OF THE LOON

Oh, we know the loon
dives down below

because we see it—
the sleek, slicked-

back black feathers
that soon emerge,

head shaking out
all the wrong ideas.

Though where it goes
is anybody's guess.

Nowhere, perhaps—
simply disappears,

like moons, loons,
yesterday, years.

TWO

THE ROPE IN THE MOTOR

Scissor-kicking, knife-wielding, I sawed
the ski rope snarled in the inboard prop,

then rose to a dock of family bystanders
broadcasting their panic like news talk,

so dove down again among the underwater
glass-green, the distant engine insect-sound,

where filaments frayed, skeins of ski rope
tore away, but each out-of-breath rise

was met with the tantalizing inquiries
of "You got it yet?" and "How bad is it?"

It was bad. A problem, partly, of guilt:
rope thrown over stern, boat in reverse,

and only I felt how tightly it hugged
the motor, only I knew how long it'd take

to undo my mistake. It took the whole hour
it would take with the therapist or priest.

Hour of anger in sunlight and lake light,
hour I confessed shallow, terrible things

beneath the surface while cutting at it—
litanies of illicit sex, the misuse of funds

from the family trust, the fact I thought
my wife a bitch. Down there it felt good

for my words to be misunderstood—
bubbles, garbling up, to where they stood.

THE OLD MAN'S DULL KNIVES

In the toolshed after his death
I angled the Buck blade
against the crude side
of the oiled whetstone
with my steady hand sweeping
rolling over
pushing the new edge into
the precisely fine degree needed
to slice through
the sandpapery skin
of a catfish
just like he showed me once
having motored out
in thick cypress
to a fish shack
before dust and sawdust
had settled over these tools
all as dull
as a story like this was
is to me
when I have taken the filet
the Bowie
the serrated one
with a compass on the bottom
and tried to hone them
back into the things they once were
oh how I am
now remembering
the fish shack
as nothing
but a plywood mess
with only an upturned mattress
and a wide-eyed rat
among the same smell of dust and sawdust
like that before me
in a toolshed

where I've run my thumb
along the beveled steel
but where things will never be
as they once were

THE HURRICANE DOOR

Rodin's Thinker did not perch above it,
nor any warning that through the door
was the way to the woeful city,

but it was closed when we moved in—
a dusty tome, its dirty-penny smell
of chipped rust. *The Gates of Hell*?

I hadn't read about them then
nor known that in our own tradition
condemned spirits are driven

downward in the basement darks,
though I'd already conjured up
one lost soul from our new home's past:

Miss Laverne Watson, widow-ghost,
recently dead in the bed upstairs,
spinster-hoarder, no Virgilian guide,

and so I found myself trying to get
inside, prying the door open,
roaming through catacombs of clutter:

grimy andirons, broken chandeliers,
dust-smeared hall mirrors bearing
briefly the dark flash of my reflection,

the toothless grin of a spread out piano,
crystal ball, bed frame, still-life prints,
biographies of all the presidents.

But I did not cry out, "Why hoard?"
or "Why squander?" like Dante's
bald-headed clerics of circle four,

for I was six, oblivious and quiet,
cocooned in cobwebbed brick.
Down there were futures

of renovation, but it was still the same
basement when Hugo hurried toward us
that September, and I remember descending—

my mother's face flashing in candle flame—
as wind whipped the world outside,
stripped the live oaks down

to a kind of wicked spiderwork,
while our dog snored on the blankets
and pawed at a nightmare.

I'd swear all throughout the night
that she was down there with us,
Miss Watson, the gray outline

of her cold face vanishing in the walls,
but they told me to be quiet and still,
then read of Van Buren, a story to fall

down into a cluttered half sleep,
where I dreamed, not knowing it,
like Dante, in a land of rain, of ascent.

THE HOUSE OF MIRRORS

Halfway through the Fun House I found myself
everywhere: swollen, withered, distorted,
stretched and skewed, face and body split in half—

body now, face then—all symmetry contorted—
uglier, fatter, skinnier, lost.
I wanted out. I knew the way ahead

was without reflection, so I tunneled past
those mocking selves to find the open spaces—
head down, arms out, fingers grazing glass.

I let myself be guided by the voices,
the shuffling of feet, the carnival laughter.
Dead-ended, I looked up to see three faces

consult each other peripherally
in a web of mirrors. Three translations,
three incorrect selves, the triple NOT ME.

They all glanced in separate directions,
as if when I turned to find the exit,
each would pursue detached ambitions

and disperse among the selves inexact
as ghosts, haunting this House of Mirrors.
So I turned. I sensed those selves diffract

like broken ice. I shut my eyes. I wanted mother.
Someone led me by the hand to air. Still,
I know the self I left behind, frozen in terror.

JUMP-START

Always now I grip the jumper clips
and with the electric neurotic spark
hear again our old mechanic, Sarge,
sitting on a ripped-up, stripped-out
pickup-cab seat at the Phillips 66,
bark: *Son, you better always remember:*
black for negative nigger, after positive
redneck red. Sometimes the trick is
to forget what's said, don't forgive,
but now, remember, Sarge is dead,
and gone the shell-shocked limp,
the chubby bald head, the charges
fired at his lackey, Wild Bill Colpini,
who, shirtless and lean as a fan belt,
drank himself to sleep each night
in a Plymouth minivan propped up
on cinder blocks behind the garage.
To forgive what's said, that's the trick,
but don't forget, remembering now
how not to get shocked bringing back
the dead. I bend in the hood shade
the way I did in the tire-pillar shadow
when Sarge and Wild Bill worked
two afternoons on my father's Ford,
hoisting the engine with a chain lift
from a live oak—*just like a lynching,*
they agreed, and who could forget
the sight of the car's heart dripping
with grease in the heat of the sun?
And who would forgive the dead
for all that they've said and done?

TO THE LITTLE GIRL ON THE HIGH DIVE
WHO WON'T JUMP DOWN

"That slows each impulse down
to indecision" PHILIP LARKIN

Though they beckon,
your expert friends
in the deep end,
or darker thoughts,
nightmares of skin
spanked hard,
there is a choice:
turn and, ushered
by the lifeguard,
climb down
the long ladder
into shame.

Even though
they chant your name—
"Su-zy! Su-zy!"—
and the diving board
seems like a tongue
joining the chorus,
and we stop our laps
to bear witness,
you (arms folded,
eyebrows knit)
wait and take
your precious time.

Suicidal
Suzy, who can't
see the likeness,
all eyes on you?
Just jump, Suzy.
But no, you wait

all day, all night,
and then it takes
ten years until
one toe edges
the line, before
you muster up
the courage to peer
over the lip
and onto the surface,
where a face
you don't remember
ever seeing
stares back.

WATERTIGHT

What would come out of her mouth,
the great-great-mute-aunt
I never heard a word
burst forth from?

Back then I didn't doubt
dust, butterflies,
the light of Jesus Christ.
For all I knew

her throat swelled up
with Socrates and I'd have sat
beside her wheelchair
as rapt as Plato.

Hummed sonatas, nonsense,
sentimental tripe?
Oh, for just one dirty joke
to come croaking out...

Summer reunions I watched her
sip Miller ponies,
then napkin-dab the droplets
bespattering her lips.

Some drunk uncle perhaps
explained it like this:
in 1917, with the Great War
beginning to ebb

across the Atlantic,
Aunt Margaret, not yet
great or even aunt-like—
sunbathing in a one-piece

on North Litchfield Beach,
lithe, loud, happy as a fish—
waded in without warning
and caught a riptide

to where they found her
sopping wet and quiet,
stretched on a sandbar
all the way by Pawleys Island.

Almost a century, always smiling,
she never disputed it,
this story, told by others,
that was her secret.

Great-great-aunt Margaret,
I want to believe it.
Tell me I'll find your voice
among the emerald islands,

or that you traded it
for a god's knowledge—
a god you can know only
floating alone in the ocean.

SEVEN MINUTES IN HEAVEN

The lock-in, they preached, was faith: doors latched,
no reason to fear the fact we were all in one place.

Rumor was, in years past, one boy ("a regular Lot")
escaped, so Thou Shalt Not Go To Sleep became

the only commandment we obeyed, staying up late,
jacked on our sleeping bags' contraband of hot Jolt.

Pairing off, we clustered together in clergy closets
while someone watched the clock and kept time:

seven minutes each. Patricia Smith chose me
because no one else was left, and for the first six minutes

nothing happened except whispered chitchat that
passed between us like we were saying the peace

in church. Me: "Well, what if we do?" Her: "Well,
they'll never know if we don't." We had a choice:

confess we'd tried something, or tried nothing—
no divine spark, no Song of Solomon, no knowing

in any Biblical sense—nihilo ex nihilo, absolute zero—
the kind of infinite nothing that frightens me still—

so I leaned over and closed my eyes and opened
my mouth and found her tongue as rough as a wafer

but still miraculous. And in those fifteen seconds
winding down in heaven, it was possible to understand

how they make a religion out of women's bodies—
Patricia Smith's mouth pulling away like the cup

at communion, leaving that bitter taste in my mouth
when we stumbled back into the light as prophets.

THREE

NO-SEE-UMS AT THE OUTDOOR BURIAL SERVICE

Send me slapping, clapping legs and neck
like a man with the Devil riding his back,
with fear and trembling of the invisible,
infinitesimal, believe-it-before-you-see-it
Almighty swarm of damnations, chaotic
as quarks, small as periods in the hymnal
until they genuflect on the arm and swell
with the blood of the host, thrash, deliver
red welts, as on a leper, miracle in reverse,
then ascend abuzz in the shrill white-noise
insect tongue drowning out the last Amen.
At home, we say "Thank God that's over,"
meaning *these troubles of the flesh* and not
our lives, as if the two were any different.

UPROOTED ROOTS

The tree toppled in the wind last night,
came crashing close, but down on no one,

cried out last night in the slam-bang wind,
that hell-bent wind cocooning us in blacked-

out rooms, and the tallest tree that toppled
and reverberated, which we found in the morning,

the roots worm-like, spilling dirt, freshly split
from the crater where they lay last night

in the late-night wind that brought them down
like a joke in my family of running jokes:

We came from something but are going nowhere.
And then the wind died down in the morning,

was cool and coming in breezily onto the branch
with the green buds and shaking them free,

and the day ahead became what to do with it,
the tree toppled out in the wind last night,

how to saw into sections this fallen thing.

DEEP WOODS DREAM ARRANGEMENT

Has come down to it: everything is lost—
spiders scrabbling over sandstone cliffs,

where runnels of creek water funnel
past a wind-fallen shagbark hickory.

High calls of some species not my own.
Fretworks of ferns laid down for lost ants.

Never to be found except here in a dream:
a naked woman sauntering over boulders

by the creek bed, an old lover in need of
anything else. When I appear, she spooks

like a deer, under heavy-hearted leaves
loosened in wind, vanished downstream.

POLAR BEAR SWIM

Layers shed, I stood fish-naked in the morning,
then sprung out as the spooked frog: nerveless,
underwater no man at all. No thing, either, of sin—

purged, cleansed, disturbing the icy surface
to rise again, whole, baptized in the name
of river, sun, and holy cold. Nothing repressed,

a body of breath, eyes peeled open not in dream
but bearing witness to this: a sky without clouds,
pines in no shadow, the river at liberty to change

course. Of course, I quickly swam to the bank,
shivering in my goose-bumped human skin,
as quickly as I'd gotten in. There, nearly bear-like

in the dry wind, or again merely the same miracle
of water, I broke either way with common sense
and jumped again. And swam out. And jumped again.

AT THE CAVE'S MOUTH

Across switchbacks, down
the mountain
to the mouth
of the cave, I wound
and found
myself as I'd hoped: alone,
far from home,
but faltering on the shadow
line and powerless to go
through to
where nothing grew
or flew or crawled into
that I knew
to be good—blind bats, newts,
no ferns, no roots—
and show me who
would go into the cave alone,
least of all return,
not the sun
which I stood under
pondering
the dark I would not enter
but that, no matter,
will come.

GHOST CRABS

Tonight coral light
from a streetlamp
spills a shadow-reef
across the floor,

and I look over
what must be
twenty years
to where my father

hooked his thumbs,
palms open,
and finger-drummed
to show a crab

sidling the wall
toward the dark hole
that was my skull.
Watch it! he cried,

and I watched
black colliding forms,
half-terrified
the crab had crawled

inside my mind
to take back
each low-tide night
we stalked the coastline

with metal bats
and flashlights,
hunting ghost crabs
that sidle wide-eyed

like stray thoughts,
casting finger shadows,
though now,
as I watch shadows

in an empty room,
shadows are letters
that spell out nonsense,
and I'm half-terrified

it's been twenty years
since my father,
alive at the bed's edge,
made what appeared

on the blank wall
outside of me
seem very real
and not real at all.

SHARK'S TOOTH

Gray gnarl sized up between the thumb
and finger, where, from any angle, I get
the point—brief pricking puncture of skin—
a *godsend*, she'd said then of the find,
when, combing the shoreline for shells,
I'd held it parallel to the sunset so that,
one eye closed, it blacked the sun out,
in focus. Now, I hardly notice it, kept
in a drawer I never open, those years,
that girl, little fin rattling and surfacing
among the letters signed *forever yours*.
Forever mine: ridged, obsidian-smooth,
dusted-off, polished rare find, the shark's
taste for blood she left in my mouth.

WITH THE WEDDING KNIFE

a gift of desert ironwood and steel

First I swiped through white onion,
teary and happy as a young husband,
and my god was it something the way
it worked my way, smooth and clean,
as sweet as what I cut through next—
haloes of green onion, green pepper,
celery that fell away into little grins
beside the sand-dollared jalapenos—
and I know you know this recipe, wife,
love of my life, rhyme bearer of knife—
the split-open bellies of baby tomatoes,
two halves, nothing whole, not even
the broccoli I chopped down, dreaming
of small trees, my wrists, your throat.

THE THIRD MAN

I was he, you said,
who was not me,
and, you said, we
were no longer us.

Tell me again, I said,
is there, or has
there ever been
another he, not me?

...Not you or he,
you said, but we
now are they who
were not yet to be.

BABYDOLL

If we had the same skin—porcelain, unbruised—
I'd be smug and chaste, too, at the top of the shelf.

We'd rule the kingdom of the little girl's bedroom
or freak away, at last, to some dusty basement box.

I am no god, and new desires have come to me.
I call out your name—*Babydoll, Babydoll*—

and wait until you gesture. What carelessness,
standing on the chair's edge to bring you down!

Come down, Babydoll. You are all I have wanted—
quiet and easy, fast, slow. No one will ever know,

any love, the two of us who share this one heart,
these sweet nothings in your little shell-like ears.

Babydoll, Babydoll, come here into my tough arms—
your delicate wrists, bonnet and dress unclasped.

Don't shy away from me. Come here, Babydoll.
It won't hurt. Babydoll, nothing could ever hurt you.

TO A DECOY

You of no coital origin, hollow mallard,
doll of all waterfowl, paint-by-numbers
boy toy disembodied from the duck call's

ventriloquistic trick, dummy's euphemism,
immaculately conceived in the work shed
where I found you junked with punctured

hip boots, rusted shotguns, spinning reels
so bird-nested they tested the last patience
I had for being outside, instead of in here,

in the poem, where point of view fixates
on you the way my eyes sometimes do
when zeroing in on the naked mannequin.

THE LIZARD-MAN

An orphaned thing, our fathers said,
in ooze and rot, stalking the swamp.

We watched for his two red eyes
like stoked coals as our flashlights

shone across the screened-in fog
of the campsite, stopped, reached

a cypress stump, like a lizard-man
that seemed to jump from the pond

and stand eerily still. Beams dimmed.
Shrill swampy night sounds rose

and closed in over the comic relief
of my cousin's first voiced thought:

Do you think it's, like, got a dick?
We hunched in our sleeping bags,

fetal-positioned, breathless with heat.
Hours later I peeked, needing to pee,

and saw the thick wall of dark woods
where the lizard man surely flicked

his forked tongue, waiting for me
to creep over and zip down for him.

THE BEAR IN THE CAMPGROUNDS

"The wounds of black bears were
found to heal during hibernation."
RAFIL KROLL-ZAIDI

Too long you sleep
beneath rigid

starless ceilings
before the bear

lumbers out of
the night forest

with its blue limbs
lurching forward

in the soft wind,
and then crosses

the riverbed,
splashing awake

the nightmare world
of appetite:

each stump sitting
in the wet earth

and each rustle
in the gold leaves

then Becoming,
but not Being,

the death-shade bear
rearing its head

without scaring,
prowling the owl-loud

campgrounds like doubt,
like dark matter,

its narrow eyes
greenly aglow

from worlds beyond,
the way stars

are distant light
from dying suns,

the way you stay
inside yourself

afterwards
the whole winter,

as bear-shade death
now heals for you.

IMAGINARY ARRANGEMENT WITHOUT SQUIRRELS

Nothing manic but mica schist glints,
flint-flaked dust motes in late light.

Black ants keep up a certain cadence,
crowding a crumb in pandemonium,

but even they refuse to act ecstatic.
Nothing chipper but cloud break's

minnow shadows swimming on soil,
the unscrewed light from the sundial,

cicadas striking up their shrill notes,
pining away. Kudzu chokes the fence,

but even it has nothing to say for itself.
The slow hand rubs the twitching eye.

All clear: nothing delirious but star-rise.

PORCH-CEILING BLUE

We rocked back, ascended into heaven—
afternoon of the wicker rocker's creak
under the overhead fan and hanging fern—

followed the jagged pitchforked crack
that scrambled the porch ceiling blue,
then withdrew into a dusk of crickets.

Shadowed occasions, love poems: too few,
you complained. I read aloud from Rilke.
You (why lie?) sighed, and we both flew

up into this illusion painted for wasps
who, in mistaking it for the infinite sky,
turn away, and do not build their nests.

Oh, you too make the end seem endless.

Hastings Hensel is the author of a previous chapbook, *Control Burn*, and the recipient of the 2014-2015 South Carolina Arts Commission Fellowship in Poetry. His poems have appeared in *storySouth*, *The Greensboro Review*, *Cave Wall*, *32 Poems*, and elsewhere. He teaches at Coastal Carolina University, where he is the poetry editor of *Waccamaw*, and lives with his wife, Lee, in Murrells Inlet, South Carolina.

Text and titles in Minion.
Cover and interior design
by Andrew Saulters.

The author signed 26 hardcover
copies, lettered A to Z. Unicorn Press
produced 75 further hardcover copies.
400 copies were bound in paper.

Titles in the Unicorn Press First Book Series

FIRST BOOK AWARD
Winter Inlet by Hastings Hensel (2014)
Earthquake Owner's Manual by Martin Arnold (2013)

EDITOR'S CHOICE
California Winter League by Chiyuma Elliott (2014)